AI-Powered Marketing: The Future of Digital Advertising

Jim Stephens

Published by RWG Publishing, 2023.

AI-POWERED MARKETING: THE FUTURE OF DIGITAL ADVERTISING

First edition. February 17, 2023.

Written by Jim Stephens.

Also by Jim Stephens

Kindle Publishing Made Easy: Autopilot Cash With Amazon Kindle!
Million-Dollar Secrets of the Amazon Associates: How They Make Money From the Biggest Online Shopping Mall
Self-Publishing Made Easy: The Easy Way to Self-publish Your Own Books!
Scam Busters: How to Avoid the Most Popular Scams of Today!
Affiliate Marketing and Blogging
The Quick and Easy Guide of Diamonds
Government Information
Hiking and Camping
Koi Pond
Law Information Guide
Motor Homes Research
Affiliate Marketing and Success Systems
Online Shopping
Outsourcing Ebooks and Software Jobs
Personal Loans
Private Jet Charters
Private Yacht Charters
Internet Marketer Alpha Dog
Networking and Social Dominance in the Twenty-First Century
Copywriting Best Kept Secrets: A Training Course for Writing Great Copy
Starting Your Home Business

Beyond Words: How ChatGPT is Revolutionizing Communication
The Language of AI: Exploring the Power of ChatGPT
Talking to Machines: The Fascinating Story of ChatGPT and AI
Language Models
Uncovering the Unknown: Tales of Mysterious Discoveries
Shadow Squadron: Inside Covert Operations
The Last Stand: The Triumph of Bravery in Desperate Times
Valor in the Skies: Courage and Sacrifice in Aerial Warfare
Courage, Sacrifice, and Honor: Tales from the Frontline Heroes

Table of Contents

Introduction

―――

Being smart about business means knowing what to expect. That means thinking ahead and preparing for the inevitable changes that will affect the way business is done. This allows businesses to be resilient and thrive in a changing environment. Digital marketing is no different.

In fact, author Josh Kaufman discusses the value of comparison in his book The Personal MBA. It means imagining possible futures and then preparing for them.

Let's say you have a large company that does well in a certain niche. Maybe you own a business that sells whey protein shakes. The mistake some big companies make is thinking they are too big to fail and sticking with it.

But what if another company comes along and makes a better protein shake for less money? What if a new protein source is discovered? What if a study showed whey protein was bad for us? All of these things can happen and can seriously disrupt even the most established business.

However, smart companies are already considering and preparing for these possibilities. It's a comparative simulation: you think about what's going to happen and then prepare for that eventuality.

As a digital marketer, this means thinking about things that might change the face of marketing. And the one thing that probably had the biggest impact of all? AI

AI and machine learning have the potential to completely change the face of internet marketing and even make many old strategies obsolete. Only by preparing for these changes can you ensure that your website can maintain its position in the SERPs, your ad campaigns remain profitable, and your services remain relevant.

And a lot of this stuff isn't just speculation: it's happening right now. AI is already making waves, though you may not have noticed it yet.

This affects how SEO works, the tools and software we use, and how ads are displayed. AI is capable of thinking faster and smarter than any human, and this is especially true for data-driven internet marketing. AI marketers can earn an unlimited amount

Content per second - doing the work of hundreds of people. All of this content is perfectly adapted to the target group. AI will rule Google. This will advance the entire business model. AdWords will start. And it will play new instruments that we never even dreamed of. The uniqueness of digital marketing is just around the corner. This book will help you prepare and explain a number of concepts:

• AI vs. machine learning

• How to do SEO now that Google is the first AI company

• Chatbots

• Programmatic advertising

• Great information

• RankBrain

• Digital assistant

• Data Science

• SQL

• Hidden semantic indexing

• The Future of Internet Marketing

This book will give you a crystal ball to look into the future of internet marketing and make sure you are prepared for all of these changes as they come. You end up being more prepared and in a better position than the other 99.9% of traders.

What is AI?

———

Before going any further, we first need to see what AI and machine learning really are. These are two related but different terms that are often confused. Both will impact marketing, but in different and unique ways.

Then AI is artificial intelligence. That means software and hardware are designed to look and act smart. Such software is capable of making meaningful decisions and performing activities that we normally think of as human responsibilities.

AI comes in two broad flavors. One of them is weak AI, also known as narrow AI. Weak AI is basically a form of AI designed to perform a specific task.

An example is a self-driving car. This form of AI is capable of knowing the position of countless cars on the road and can react by steering, accelerating, braking, etc. If you saw a self-driving car from the outside, you might think a human was driving it. In this way, he is doing work that is normally seen as a human role.

BUT at the same time, you can't talk to a self-driving car and ask it how it feels. Self-driving cars will definitely fail the Turing test!

Note: The Turing test is a test to measure AI performance. If you talk to an AI in a chat app and don't know it's not human, it's considered "passing the Turing test". Another example of weak AI being used in creating villains in computer games. They use programming to behave in a human way and challenge players.

However, the code is only useful in the context of video games, so it won't be Skynet anytime soon!

Weak AI may not sound very appealing, but it is used for some very interesting things

– from helping to cure illnesses to boosting the economy.

In contrast, the type of AI we often see in science fiction is what we know as "general AI". This is AI that doesn't just have one purpose, but is designed to do anything a human can do

make. So you can play word games with this AI, ask her how she's feeling, or ask her to find something useful.

A common AI example is DeepMind, which is owned by Google. DeepMind is a company that has developed a "neural network" that uses a "general learning algorithm" to learn many different skills.

Many AIs, such as IBM Watson, are actually pre-programmed. This means they work with some sort of flowchart and always answer questions with the same answer. On the other hand, DeepMind seems to be able to think and react through "convolutional neural networks". Certain behaviors will be reinforced and encouraged, and they will become more prominent.

It's not a perfect simulation of how the human brain works (cognitive-behavioral psychology teaches us the importance of having internal dialogue and mindsets), but it's close to "true" general intelligence.

machine learning

Machine learning, on the other hand, works differently. Machine learning uses huge data sets to create surprising and sometimes almost terrifying skills.

Machine learning basically allows software to be "trained". A vivid example of this is computer vision.

Computer vision describes the ability of some machines to understand visual information. An example is Google Lens, which can tell you what you point at with your phone's camera, whether it's a type of flower or a product you can buy in a store. Computer vision is required by self-driving cars to successfully navigate their surroundings and is used by apps like Snapchat, which uses filters to change people's faces.

How does it work? By looking at thousands and thousands of photos of all kinds of objects. While a machine learning algorithm never knows what it's looking at, it can look for patterns in the data, which are then useful for future identification of that object. For example, he may notice that the face is usually oval in shape, with a patch of black hair on top. Then he knew he was probably looking at a face when he saw an oval with a dark dot above it.

Machine learning has great potential in almost every field. In the future, it could diagnose disease more accurately than human doctors, advise on financial decisions, detect bank transfer fraud and more.

All of this has HUGE potential implications for internet marketing, and that is what we will explore in the following chapters.

Google An AI Company

Some time ago, Google announced that it has become the first company with AI. While this may sound like meaningless marketing bullshit, the truth is that this provision actually has HUGE potential implications for marketers, businesses, and SEO.

First, what does Google mean by that?

Meet the new, smarter Google

Perhaps the first thing you think of is Google as a search company. The first product provided by Google was a search engine, and that is what most of us still associate with the company.

Traditionally, Google's search engine doesn't work as much as AI does. Instead, search works by trying to match search terms to article content. Because of this, SEO experts have been advised to include lots of key phrases in their articles so that Google's spiders can read this content and quickly see that it matches what the person is looking for.

As we all know, this didn't work out perfectly for Google. Many unscrupulous "marketers" abuse the system by stuffing hundreds of search terms into each article, which in turn causes the content that Google displays to users to be garbled and unreadable.

Because of this, Google started to work more like AI over time. Now Google no longer tries to find exact match keywords. Instead, Google tries to answer the questions you ask. This is done by trying to understand what users are looking for in context and then providing relevant answers through their searches.

RankBrain

Google can do this through machine learning. Specifically, it uses a form of natural language processing that Google calls RankBrain.

RankBrain is at least partly responsible for helping Google deal with never-before-seen phrases and words. When RankBrain identifies a word it doesn't recognize, it can "guess" what it means based on context and how it's used elsewhere. This helps Google deal with unusual searches it hasn't seen before, without simply matching search terms to content in articles.

Search queries are converted into "word vectors" which are called "distributed representations". These are words and phrases that are close together in meaning and context. RankBrain then tries to map the query to words it understands or groups of similar words. From here, it gets what the searcher actually meant and was looking for, and returns results based on that. RankBrain also understands the relationship between words and how they work together.

In the past, conjunctions like "the" or "and" were ignored by Google. Google now understands what this phrase means and how it affects user intent.

Like all the best machine learning algorithms, RankBrain tries to improve over time and adapt to users. He can see which results are clicking the most, so he knows when he's doing well and when he's doing something wrong. As such, it can quickly improve search results for certain keywords through algorithmic testing, which helps weed out low-quality content that tries to trick the system.

RankBrain works with Tensor Processing Units (TPU), AI-only hardware housed in Google's data centers. These are specialized chips that can better handle the specific challenges of machine learning tasks.

Google Extras Plan

In recent years, Google may have diversified. Now it's making smartphones, now it's making self-driving cars, and now it's making apps like Google Lens.

But at the heart of all these initiatives is some form of AI, or machine learning. Google Lens uses machine learning to identify objects in a scene and allows users to "see" the real world around them. Self-driving cars, of course, rely heavily on various forms of AI.

And Google Pixel phones? You could say their main focus is putting Google Assistant in everyone's pocket.

And that's the real clue as to what Google is doing. Google Assistant is an AI and virtual assistant that allows users to get weather forecasts, order taxis, play music and much more. The Google Assistant uses a combination of machine learning (to recognize human speech, for example) and AI to produce useful results and speak naturally.

Google Assistant is tightly integrated with Google Search. You can ask Google Assistant questions like "Who is in Iron Man?" and it will give you a natural answer. It does this by first using machine learning to turn your speech into strings, then using Google search to find useful answers (including machine learning in the form of RankBrain), and then using narrow AI to extract the most helpful answers from above. web page and then uses another form of narrow AI to provide answers in a natural sounding way (designed to look like general AI). A lot of this doesn't happen on the device you're talking about, but on Google's TPUs being in the cloud.

What does all this mean for marketers?

What does all this mean for marketers? Simple: it means that Google wants to be able to understand your content and extract the most useful information. He no longer wants you to use difficult keywords and wants you to set up a harder search form.

Google relies heavily on AI and machine learning. Believes AI assistant will be BIG in the future and wants Google Assistant to be number one. He envisions a future where we spend less time staring at our devices and instead get the information we need by asking our phones or Google Homes. We will of course talk to these devices and they will give us useful answers.

Semantic Search

W hether Google Assistant is Google's intended ubiquitous tool or not, the fact remains that Google wants search to be more natural and human. Already in many ways.

This means that marketers and website owners need to make some changes to how they work. Finding keywords and repeating them many times is no longer enough, now you have to work as if you were talking to AI. And that means a number of things.

LSI: Latent Semantic Indexing

Latent Semantic Indexing is one of the most important things to consider if you are interested in improving your SEO and getting to the top of Google. It's even more important if you hope to be ready for Google's AI-driven future. This is not only a powerful concept in its own right, but an important microcosm of the broader changes we see in SEO today.

Search engine optimization is a big and very important part of digital marketing and if you want to drive the maximum number of people to your website or blog then having a search engine is very important.

In the past, SEO relied heavily on creating lots of content on a particular topic and repeatedly using a number of keywords or key phrases in that content to help Google identify the topic and help the right visitors find your page. Unfortunately, some people start taking advantage of this system and start "keyword stuffing" by using the same keywords over and over to get annoying. Google needs to get smarter, and it is working.

Right now, overusing the same keywords will get you into trouble. What does Google do? It examines the wider context and topic of the article. In other words, it searches for synonyms and related terms, which also provides a better understanding of what your page is about.

For example, if you write an article about "decision trees", then in the past Google could theoretically get confused and return your page as a result when someone searches the tree. He might think you're talking about decisions about trees!

However, it can now search for related terms such as "flowchart" and thus help assign articles to readers more precisely. LSI actually comes from mathematics and uses a technique called singular value decomposition. This means scanning unstructured data and looking for relationships between words and concepts in it.

Dealing with LSIs

So how do you ensure your website is LSI optimized? Short answer: you don't.

While it's definitely tempting for SEO companies to start offering their LSI optimized services now, the truth is you should do this without a second thought. This is what top web marketing experts like Andrei Ilysin and Matt Cutts always recommend.

In short, natural writing should mean you include synonyms and related subjects. Otherwise, your writing will sound very repetitive. As always, the moral is: stop guessing and just write for readers! We'll keep coming back here as we gear up for a smarter Google.

But there are a few other tips you can keep in mind if you want to make sure Google knows what you're talking about.

First, make sure you use more than one search term. We recommend using different combinations of search terms rather than just targeting one, for several reasons. Because Google often returns results that don't use the exact keyword phrase you're looking for, it makes sense to include some popular repetitions of the same term.

You should also pay attention to a good and varied vocabulary on the topic. This helps to better present the context and topic of your article. Instead of filling the article with random synonyms, think of words that come up frequently with the topic you're working on (like our previous block diagram example). I like it!

structured data

Another big concept that SEO needs to consider to be ready for Google's AI in the future is schema markup, aka structured data, aka rich data.

Remember: Google's goal is to enable Assistant to answer natural language questions with useful answers based on information found on the web. In addition to displaying a useful list of search results, Google wants to be able to answer questions. So when someone asks how to make bolognese, they just read the ingredients.

To do this, Google has to be able to find the most relevant information in a text and then take a specific answer. This takes the RankBrain concept to the next level, enabling him to understand not only what an article is about, but also how each paragraph in the article works.

The problem is Google's AI can't do that just yet. At least not good enough to provide people with useful answers without occasionally containing gibberish!

This is where schematic markers come into play.

Basically, the idea behind schema markup is to annotate your articles and blog posts, telling Google what it is every bit of and what it does. You're basically saying "Here is an ingredient list" or "Here is a user review".

It also helps Google to provide what it calls "extended snippets". Expanded snippets are search results in SERPs (search engine results pages) that contain more than just a meta description. You might see search results that also include bulleted steps or ingredients for that dish, for example. This allows users to view the information they are looking for without leaving this website!

How to use markup

Markup is very similar to HTML. Here's an example of how it looks:

This actually tells Google that you are talking about a local business (Candle Factory). You can also use schemas to tag product names, authors, summary reviews, software applications, restaurants, movies and more!

To use it yourself, you can either browse the HTML and implement it yourself, or use Google's handy markup helper: https://www.google.com/webmasters/markup-helper/u/0/.

Here you simply share the URL of the page you want to tag and then you have the option to create the required tags.

There are also plugins that you can use in WordPress for the same purpose.

Pros and cons of schema markup

The experienced among you may have noticed some worrisome issues with schema markup. Specifically: You encourage people not to visit your website!

Let's say you have a website with recipes and articles about Bolognese. You might do this with the hope that people will Google it, find your site, and then visit your page to read more about it. That way they might as well click on some ads, buy affiliate products, or just remember your brand so they'll come back in the future.

But if Google just takes your key information and passes it on, then there's no real incentive for them to actually visit your website. Therefore, they don't have the opportunity to click on your ads or buy your products. They won't even know that the information came from your website!

Therefore, in effect, Google uses our intellectual property without any compensation - which has angered many webmasters, companies and marketers.

So should you avoid this feature altogether? Unfortunately, that's not really an option. Keep in mind that Google also uses markup to provide rich snippets. These are media-rich search lists that contain things like star ratings, images, points, and more. They really help websites stand out in the SERPs, thereby getting more people to click on those listings.

And while you may not get any benefit from Google reading your materials, if you don't use a markup language, Google is simply getting the same information from one of your competitors. Google wants us to use schema markup, and that means it's more likely to reward pages that can do a bit of an SEO boost. For all of these reasons, it's important that you continue to use this strategy, even if you may be providing free information to Google in this way.

In the future, if more and more people start talking to their Google Assistant instead of scouring the web for information, it's possible Google will have to reconsider its policy: don't face a sizable backlash from content creators!

Big Data

You may often hear the term "big data" and not quite understand what it means. In this chapter you will enlighten and learn how big data can help you and your business now and in the future.

Big data is basically nothing more than large amounts of data. These large amounts of data are increasingly common online because everything is easy to measure and document online. When you think of companies like Google, they have huge datasets to work with, detailing the search history of billions of users.

But even a standard website with 1,000 visitors per day will handle large amounts of information. The website will of course log each of these visits and also store data about each visit - such as country of origin and time spent on the website. In a few weeks, this data will likely crash many spreadsheet programs!

The reason Big Data is included in so much discussion is because it is so difficult to deal with. Understanding large amounts of information requires a lot of clever math, while simply storing and processing this type of data requires a lot of storage space and computing power.

But the potential value of big data is also enormous. Big data provides patterns and insights that you can't get by observing multiple users. This is basically how machine learning works – by looking for patterns in very large data sets. The difference is that it is used in a slightly different way.

predictive modeling

Predictive modeling is a process that involves mining data and probabilities to predict potential future outcomes. The model is built using a set of "predictors". Predictors are variables that are expected to influence future outcomes.

Once data about these predictors is collected, a statistical model can be built. It can use simple linear equations or complex neural networks. After all, statistical analysis can be used to make predictions about how things will develop in the future.

In terms of marketing, it can contribute to better customer insights, better lead scores, campaign support, up and cross selling, personalized product recommendations and much more!

Amazon is an example of a website that uses big data to provide personalized product recommendations. Amazon not only uses a database of grouped items (which can be difficult to maintain), but also automatically generates data from each transaction and sale, then looks for patterns. It will see what products are usually bought together (there are those concurrent occurrences again) so it can use that information to display items it thinks the next user might want to buy!

Big data can also be very useful when assessing prospects. Scoring leads means understanding which prospects are likely to be ready to buy and which are not. This is especially useful information for businesses looking to send sales letters to cross sections of their mailing lists that they believe will actually buy from them (instead of being put off by the amount of marketing materials they receive).

Amnesty International uses segmentation techniques and predictive modeling to better identify the right groups for marketing. By collecting the data and then seeing what the data says about the type of donor, Amnesty International knows who to target with its advertising, how likely they are to spend and how likely they are to do so.

Any charity can benefit from this type of data analysis, as can any business.

Big data collection

If you want to start collecting data for your business, there are a number of plugins and tools you can use to do this. You should find that many tools like Google Analytics allow you to export large amounts of data for use.

They can then use this information themselves or outsource it to data science organizations who can use this information to provide valuable and useful information.

Another great idea to be prepared for the future is allowing users to create profiles. This allows you to collect more data about individual users and also provide better individual recommendations in the future. This is something stores have been doing with loyalty cards for decades, but of course the digital nature of selling online creates even more potential!

Computer Training

———

As previously mentioned, computer vision is the ability of machines and computers to "see" by learning from large data sets and machine learning. By observing countless images, a machine can learn to identify images in an object or navigate the environment without bumping into things.

What does this mean for the future of SEO?

One BIG thing - and one thing you need to be prepared for - is that Google will likely pay more attention to images on websites.

Traditionally, we've been told to avoid using images for things like website names. Why? Because Google cannot "read" and render and therefore we have no SEO advantage over it.

But Google has software that can read text from an image. It's called OCR (Optical Character Recognition), and if you want to see how good it is, try hovering over Google Translate at a foreign language and see it appear real-time in your native language. If Google can do that, then it's only a matter of time before it starts reading the text in your images to see if they support the niche and keyword phrases you're targeting with your site.

With facial recognition already playing such a big role in security and Facebook, it may only be a matter of time before Google uses it too.

For example, if you write a blog post about Sylvester Stallone, Google may one day not only look at your content, but also the photos on your page to see if there are any photos of Stallone! Google Images may one day stop relying on surrounding text altogether, instead basing its results solely on what's in the image and whether it matches what you're looking for.

Topics like image quality are also likely to play a major role going forward. Google may choose not to recommend your website if it thinks the images there are poorly chosen and out of place.

So what can you do to prepare? So far, the closest thing to communicating with Google through images is using markup and/or filenames and alt tags. Using alt tags to describe an image can help Google recognize what it is and therefore better decide whether your site is suitable for a particular user.

In the meantime, make sure the images you use are relevant and of high quality!

Advertising

———

At its core, machine learning is about development. It's about getting more data to the point where more accurate claims can be made. While recognizing faces in images can start out badly, the system evolves and learns until it becomes more accurate than humans.

Imagine being able to turn that power into advertising. Imagine being able to show the right ad to the right person at the right time. Imagine if your ad campaign "evolved" to become more specific, so that more viewers clicked on your ad and bought your product. The longer the campaign lasts, the more your profits increase and the less you spend on ineffective advertising.

That's how programmatic advertising works, and you can get started right away!

What is programmatic advertising?

Programmatic advertising campaigns allow marketers to purchase native ads across various publisher sites, using intelligent algorithms to ensure they are targeting the right audience at the right time while staying on budget, thanks to a bidding system that allows them to compete with other advertisers to compete for impressions.

In short, these campaigns provide the precision and quality of native advertising (such as banner ads) while allowing for the control, customization, and precision that you'll get with PPC campaigns. The end result is ads that appear on carefully selected publisher websites, but only as and when they are likely to produce the best results.

Programmatic advertising uses complex algorithms to identify your company's ideal customers and then understand where they are likely to appear on the web. It then displays ads in those locations and then uses learning algorithms to do so

Instead of going from publisher to publisher discussing prices, let a "bot" do all the work for you. More importantly, don't waste money on ad space that no one sees. Your ads are selected and refined by intelligent algorithms and as a result, achieve a higher CTR with the right target customers!

RTB

This is how programmatic buying is different from PPC, or simply buying a banner ad on your favorite news site. Meanwhile, the option to use RTB or "real-time bidding" gives you added control.

What RTB basically means is that every time a page is loaded, you automatically enter a bidding war based on your pre-set budget. This bidding contest allows your ad to compete with other advertisers across different websites that suit the particular demographics and contexts you have chosen. In other words, you're indicating that you want to target sports websites that cater to a male audience in their 20s-40s, and from there your ads will appear on a selection of those sites (some of which you can still manage). case, if desired) based on the outcome of each small bid. This way you can target your audience to a variety of different websites and avoid paying too much for them).

On the other hand, a direct buy is basically a large order of impressions from one or more specific sites like ESPN. You can still filter impressions based on a number of factors, such as: B. location or browser, but basically you're targeting specific websites and securing a spot in that exact location.

Direct Buy is effectively a bit more like banner ads, while RTB is a bit more like the PPC model, where you bid for space on multiple sites (while still having more control).

Deciding what is best for you depends on a number of factors. For example, your budget will play a role because buying outright is usually more expensive (due to lower CPI's not much of a chance to get started). Also, remember that RTB gives you more flexibility, more data, and more control - you can determine which sites work best for you, at what times, and for which audiences, then customize your approach further.

However, if you bid too low with your RTB, you run the risk of not showing your ad at all. This is in direct contrast to an outright purchase, which is essentially "guaranteeing" your ad space and you are ultimately guaranteed to receive that number of impressions. This is useful for companies with more specific goals and tight schedules. Likewise, direct purchases give you more control over where ads appear and create a closer relationship between your brand and the publisher's brand.

Therefore, different approaches work for different traders and for different purposes. It's your job to decide what's best for you, and the best way to do that might be to jump in and try it for yourself.

How to Improve Your Programmatic Purchasing Results

Programmatic advertising is a crucial new tool for any company looking to expand its customer base and has very quickly gained popularity in the online marketing sector. Yet, even the best programming tools are only as good as the people using them, so before you jump to conclusions, take into account these four essential suggestions to guarantee your success.

Don't forget about the creative component

It doesn't matter how targeted your ad is or how smart your campaign is in terms of exposure, if you haven't invested in the creative aspect, the ad will fail. Design your ad well and test which design works best. Also, think about your brand identity and how you can reinforce it with non-clickable ads as well. Choose a program partner who can support you in this aspect.

Consider the audience and the context

Before choosing which publisher to work with, you need to consider the audience they are appealing to and the context. The ideal partner is a website that writes about topics related to yours and targets the exact same audience that you are targeting.

However, in some cases, you can't find both, so you should choose the publisher that offers the best balance. And don't be tempted to ignore context in such situations, as research shows those same people are more likely to click on golf club ads on golf websites than on news sites. Specifically, someone who wants a wedding dress is only going to want that wedding dress at a certain point in their life, and this really goes to show how important context is.

Be prepared to spend money in advance

The advantage of programmatic advertising is that you can instantly manage your spending in real-time to ensure you get maximum exposure no matter what your budget. However, it is highly recommended to start with a higher spending limit than you are willing to continue with, as this will help you identify what is working and what is not. Remember, you want more data and that means you want more clicks. Optimizing your campaign based on statistics and ROI will bring you closer to an optimal setup, but if you don't spend money up front, you can't know if your campaign is successful because you won't win enough bids. Spend a little upfront and once you get into your groove, you'll save money in the long run.

Make sure your ads are relevant

The downside to any automated ad campaign is that you can lose that 'personal touch' - the benefit of working with publishers to develop ad campaigns that match the tone and look of their entire site and broadcast them anywhere to promote their content.

Unfortunately, native advertising is difficult to measure, which is why so many automated platforms are popular.

To be successful with programmatic advertising, you need to keep this in mind. Your ad will be targeted to the right people, on the right device, in the right context. But is it right for the job? These ads should look like native ads, just like banner ads. Creating ads integrated into a series of "neighborhoods" is one way to do this. Another way is to choose a tool that allows you to choose the brand you want to work with and then choose the brand that already aligns with your own goals and style.

Email Marketing

The key to online success is not just getting traffic, but controlling that traffic. What does that mean? That means you need to know how to decide which visitor you're going to talk to at any given time. This means you need to understand your visitors and know what they are thinking, what their mood is and what they are interested in at the moment. And that means knowing how and when to take action when selling a product or encouraging people to sign up for your mailing list. This is a theme that comes up again and again in machine learning and AI. And email marketing is no different.

You can do all of this by creating mailing lists and then segmenting the lists.

First, let's discuss the basics of email marketing again for those who are not familiar.

Email marketing, of course, is the process of marketing via email. In other words, it means you create a large list - a collection of emails - and do so by asking your website visitors to share their contact details when they land on your homepage.

This in turn requires an automated response. Autoresponders are tools you use to create email forms and then manage all the contacts on your list. You can use a form anywhere on your page to have people fill in their details, and you use autoresponders to actually send all of your emails.

It should be immediately clear what value it has. Sending all your e-mails manually using Gmail or any other web client is not easy and will most likely result in many undelivered e-mails. You will have to send many different emails for longer lists and manage all subscription or unsubscribe requests manually.

The autoresponder does everything for you, so all you have to do is compose an email and then click send. However, another benefit of an autoresponder is that it can collect data about you and use that information for a number of different things. For example, an autoresponder can show you the percentage of subscribers who actually opened your email. If your email subject line isn't getting people to read, you can identify the problem and fix it.

Suddenly we're using a data-driven approach and machine learning again!

You can then see all the visitors who have read the message in one place. Or choose to see everyone who isn't. You can view open rates for different unique visitors and organize your list based on various factors.

This is another useful thing about using autoresponders: they allow you to capture more information with forms embedded in your pages, and that information can then be used to segment your visitors. Do you only want to message boys? Do. Only want to message people over 30? You can do this too. Or how about a few different mailing lists for different brands or even different products? All of this can be achieved with just one autoresponder.

And of course, this kind of control and automation opens up all kinds of possibilities for marketers when it comes to AI and machine learning.

Lead email warmth and segmentation

The real power of all this information is that you can use it to choose who to direct your message to. For example, you may decide that you only want to email people who fall into certain categories.

What we're interested in to begin with is sending emails based on engagement, retention, and warmth.

A lead is anyone who has shown an interest in buying from you. This means anyone who has subscribed to your mailing list can be considered a prospect simply because they have shown interest.

But at the same time, anyone who visits your website or picks up your card is also a potential customer. This is a "cold" lead, while someone actually giving you their contact information is a "warm" lead.

The hotter the prospects are, the more interested they are in what you do and what you sell. And the warmer it looks, the more likely they will buy from you.

In fact, that's the real and most profitable purpose of mailing list building: it lets you take cold prospects and turn them into warm prospects and then paying customers.

I always compare this to asking someone for their phone number. If you just walked up to someone at a club and asked for their number, they would likely just tell you to leave.

Why would they give you their number if they know nothing about you and show no interest in you?

First you need to talk to them and let them get to know you. If they look at you and smile, they are a cold trail. If they respond to your witty banter by telling you their name, they'll take the lead. If they have kissed you or allowed you to buy them a drink, they are an interesting lead. And once it's hot, you can ask for their number.

It's all about timing. The timing is wrong and they don't give you their number because you didn't lay the groundwork!

The same goes for internet marketing. If someone visits your website and you tell them to buy your product immediately, they won't. Why should they? You don't give them any reason to trust you. You haven't told them anything about yourself. You don't know much about the product.

Ask them to submit their email address after a few blog posts and you can gently start increasing engagement. Then you surprise them with all your information and all your knowledge. You cheer him up a bit and let him get to know you.

If they don't open your e-mail, it's akin to being cold to you. It's like the girl or boy in the club who doesn't laugh at your jokes and keeps looking the other way. Now if you try to sell to them you are spamming. And you delete yourself.

And they never come back to your website.

But when they open your email, you know you stand a chance. That means you can then send them a little more information about your product and get them excited about your launch. If they keep opening your emails during this time, you know you have a better chance of success. If you try to sell to them now, they will likely buy from you.

Email segmentation lets you do just that: You can see which visitors actually opened your emails, actually clicked on your links, and scrolled down.

With the help of cookies it is even possible to see which visitors have visited your website and viewed your products. You can see who hovered over your product and tried to click buy.

Email segmentation is coupled with machine learning

If you've been paying close attention, you probably already know where this is going. Remember when we talked about big data we said you could use predictive analytics to better assess your prospects?

This is where things can get really interesting for autoresponders in the future. Imagine if your autoresponders not only segmented your audience and looked at open and engagement rates, but also looked for trends in huge data sets.

In other words, what if your autoresponder kept track of everyone who bought from you and knew what action they usually took first. This will allow machine learning algorithms to better recognize when a user is acting like someone ready to buy and send them a customized message to encourage that purchase!

This can be combined with smart recommendations to further increase the likelihood of a purchase.

It's already being used by several big brands, so it's only a matter of time before more of us get access to that same level of precision.

Tips marketers can follow now

For all of this to work, you also need to make sure people are actually subscribing to your mailing list. It will also help us prepare for an AI-driven future. There are several ways to encourage this.

First, make sure you show your mailing list wherever you can. This should at least mean that your mailing list appears at the bottom of your posts. But at the same time, you can also place it in a sidebar so that your listing is visible on every page of your website.

Another tip is to draw attention to this. The mistake a lot of people make is creating their mailing list and then just "hoping" that people will see it. It's much more effective to occasionally tell people about it and explain in your post why this is a great opportunity and why people should be excited to sign up.

Here's the thing: You always have to be honest.

The goal of a mailing list is not to inflate it as much as possible. Rather, the aim is to increase it as much as possible with only very targeted visitors.

If your visitors are not interested in what you have to offer through your list then you will only disappoint them and spam them effectively.

Chatbots

C hatbots are an increasingly popular tool for marketers, business owners and webmasters. So what are chatbots?

In essence, a chatbot is a miniature AI that normally sits on a website and is then able to answer questions and engage in simple conversations.

Chatbots are very frequently used in customer service. In this way, websites can answer frequently asked questions and relieve customer service significantly. Companies can offer buyers the support they want without spending a fortune on additional staff and call centers.

But chatbots can be much more than customer support. Chatbots are just as effective at marketing and can be very effective at increasing sales and profits. Chatbots are very effective at starting the sales process by welcoming website visitors and asking them what they are looking for. Instead of relying on UX to try to direct visitors to the right half of a page, chatbots can ask them what they want to buy and then direct them to that page. Additionally, it can provide useful recommendations (perhaps based on past purchase history) and allay consumer concerns.

Chatbots can even get information from customers by asking them about their budget or what they are looking for. Even if they don't buy, you already understand their point and can use the information to further refine your marketing strategy.

Some experts claim that in the next few years, 85% of business will be done through chatbots! So how can you get started? 80% of companies say they want to use a chatbot in 2020!

Facebook Chat

One option is to invest in a Facebook chatbot. There are many websites and online services that will set it up for you.

Facebook Messenger is the new frontier for many small businesses. While it has slipped under the radar for many marketers, the numbers speak for themselves. Facebook Messenger is currently used by more than

1.2 billion people! That is 11% of the total human population.

And what makes Messenger even more powerful is that it can be embedded into your website. More than 20 million sites use messaging and that number is growing. It provides a very simple and easy way to communicate with your visitors, answer their questions and help convert traffic to sales.

But you can't be available 24/7 to take care of every need of your visitors. And this is where chatbots come in. It's basic AI that can take care of your customers and help you provide a more personalized experience when answering basic questions.

This is a very powerful tool for business because you will never again lose visitors having trouble navigating the site or getting the information they need.

Imagine if customers could order food by simply sending a message on Facebook and then answering a few automated questions?

Or what if a company could access your expert legal advice without having to talk to you in person? All this is possible in the near future.

Facebook chatbots can even be proactive by sending messages to potential customers. You have to be very careful with this as it can be considered spam. But when you have an automated system capable of reaching prospects at the right time with carefully crafted messages, it can be huge for business!

Another type of chatbot

Of course, not all chatbots are Facebook chatbots. There are many other ways to implement chatbots on a website, from building them from scratch with custom software to using them to reply to emails or SMS.

Develop your AI skills

If you want to make sure you don't get left behind by developments in AI and machine learning, it might be worth learning the relevant skills that you can use to implement your own strategy. At least if you understand the tools used in AI and machine learning, you will be able to explore these new horizons and make smarter decisions for your business.

One of the key concepts to understand is SQL. SQL stands for Structured Query Language and is a declarative language for storing and retrieving information from databases. If that sounds like gibberish, it basically offers a set of commands you can use to manipulate large amounts of data.

SQL is essential for data science and machine learning. It takes several forms like MySQL, SQL Server and SQLite. Each uses a slightly different dialect to achieve the same thing: interact with a relational database.

A relational database consists of several tables like you see in Excel, with columns and rows. So if you have a list of visitors to your website, you can enter their data in rows, e.g. For example name, age, contact details, etc. Pull in a visitor and it will display their details so you are ready to call and shop from them.

You can then use SQL, for example, to create entirely new tables or insert new rows, columns or cells. You can do this with simple commands like "CREATE TABLE" and "INSERT INTO".

To create a new database you must first use the command to create it and from there you can start inserting tables like this:

CREATE TABLE CLIENTS (

ROWID INTEGER PRIMARY KEY, LASTNAME TEXT,

FIRSTNAME TEXT, PHONE TEXT, EMAIL TEXT

);

One of the more powerful commands is something called SELECT which lets you retrieve information in one or more tables. For example, you could use this to get details about people over a certain age, like this:

SELECT FIRSTNAME FROM CLIENTS WHERE AGE > 23;

GROUP BY is a command that allows you to group results based on certain conditions. CURSOR lets us browse through records and make changes.

Although all this seems very simple, these simple commands combined with large amounts of data can produce interesting results and are very useful for making future decisions. This is basically how machine learning works, and if you want to work as a data scientist to deploy big data solutions or machine learning applications, here's what you need to know.

How to Safe Proof Your Marketing

———

T hroughout this eBook, we have discussed different types of AI and machine learning in the context of digital marketing.

All of this is designed to help you better prepare for the future. You know you need to start collecting as much data as possible quickly, you need to add schema markup to your website, you need to use LSI, you need to be able to use chatbots...

You even know a little bit about SQL if you ever decide to get involved behind the scenes! But all of that is likely to change a lot more before it emerges – and we can't predict exactly how that impact will feel.

There is a huge ripple going through internet marketing and the power of AI really cannot be underestimated. For example, imagine what would happen if artificial intelligence capable of writing high-quality content became commonplace and commercially available. This technology already exists — AI that can type almost like a human — but if allowed to spread across the web, it could potentially flood the web with enough new content to double or triple its size in a matter of days!

How do we know what was written by humans and what was not? What if AI could create realistic-looking images? We've seen the power of deepfakes: how do we know what's real and what's not?

We can't really prepare for this scenario because we don't know how it will turn out. So for now, it's best to focus on what we know. Specifically, as a marketer, this means focusing on Google's shift to natural language processing and more human interaction.

It also means that Google is getting smarter. Google used to look for keyword matches, but now it really understands the importance of a website and can use more metrics to determine if it's high or low quality and if it's what it says on the tin.

In fact, Google may have the potential to become the world's most powerful AI thanks to the vast amount of information it has access to and the huge resources the company invests in it. This makes it even more difficult to "stake" the system or try to trick Google.

The best thing we can do then? Create the highest quality content possible. As Google becomes more human, writing for Google and writing for readers basically mean the same thing. It's time to focus on quality content and provide real value.

The most important thing to remember is that Google serves its customers first. Who are your customers? Users who use it to seek information and entertainment. Google wants people to keep using its search, so it needs to make sure it only displays the most relevant and interesting information.

As long as you are interested in creating quality content for your readers, your goals and Google's goals will align. That way, every time you get a little smarter, it will benefit you instead of being something to worry about.

As Google gets smarter, it finds more ways to identify the best quality content. So if you focus on getting it across, Google will find more ways to connect you with your audience.

Combine that with more data collection and a generally more data-driven approach to marketing, and you're well on your way to the future of the industry.

Also by Jim Stephens

Kindle Publishing Made Easy: Autopilot Cash With Amazon Kindle!
Million-Dollar Secrets of the Amazon Associates: How They Make
Money From the Biggest Online Shopping Mall
Self-Publishing Made Easy: The Easy Way to Self-publish Your Own
Books!
Scam Busters: How to Avoid the Most Popular Scams of Today!
Affiliate Marketing and Blogging
The Quick and Easy Guide of Diamonds
Government Information
Hiking and Camping
Koi Pond
Law Information Guide
Motor Homes Research
Affiliate Marketing and Success Systems
Online Shopping
Outsourcing Ebooks and Software Jobs
Personal Loans
Private Jet Charters
Private Yacht Charters
Internet Marketer Alpha Dog
Networking and Social Dominance in the Twenty-First Century
Copywriting Best Kept Secrets: A Training Course for Writing Great
Copy
Starting Your Home Business

Affiliate Marketing for Beginners: You Will Never Succeed Unless You Take The Opportunity

A Guide to Creating the Most Appropriate Budgets for You: Additional Cash in Your Pocket

Various Advantages of Membership Websites: With Membership Websites, Create a Passive Income

Affiliate Marketing Made Simple: Avoid Common Errors and Thrive in Successes

Article Marketing Made Simple: It Is Not Necessarily Difficult to Succeed

Blogging Made Simple: Blogging Can Be Lucrative

Advertising That Pays: Increase Your Traffic and Leads

The Complete Guide to Copywriting: Creating Words That Sell

Affiliate Marketing Made Simple

The Affiliate Marketer's Manual

Aquarium Maintenance Made Simple

Beginner's Guide to Online Video Marketing

Blogging Fundamentals: Blogging is the Next Big Thing

Techniques for Advanced Search Engine Optimization: On Autopilot, Increase Your Traffic and Profits!

Article Marketing Secrets

Beginner's Guide to Black Hat SEO

Super Guide to Snowmobiling: The Best Places to Have a Great Time

Forest Adventure With Friends: A Captivating Story With a Lot of Fun

How to Advertise Like a Pro

My Journey Through Life: A Personal Memoir

The Art of Crafting Short Stories: A Guide to Writing and Publishing

The Ultimate Guide to Making Money Online: Proven Strategies and Tips for Success

Battlefield of Honor: Bravery and Sacrifice Tested In Ultimate Battle

Echoes of the Past: Unveiling History's Secrets

Warrior's Code: The Unbreakable Ethics of a Warrior

AI-Powered Marketing: The Future of Digital Advertising

Beyond Words: How ChatGPT is Revolutionizing Communication
The Language of AI: Exploring the Power of ChatGPT
Talking to Machines: The Fascinating Story of ChatGPT and AI
Language Models
Uncovering the Unknown: Tales of Mysterious Discoveries
Shadow Squadron: Inside Covert Operations
The Last Stand: The Triumph of Bravery in Desperate Times
Valor in the Skies: Courage and Sacrifice in Aerial Warfare
Courage, Sacrifice, and Honor: Tales from the Frontline Heroes

About the Publisher

Accepting manuscripts in the most categories. We love to help people get their words available to the world.

Revival Waves of Glory focus is to provide more options to be published. We do traditional paperbacks, hardcovers, audio books and ebooks all over the world. A traditional royalty-based publisher that offers self-publishing options, Revival Waves provides a very author friendly and transparent publishing process, with President Bill Vincent involved in the full process of your book. Send us your manuscript and we will contact you as soon as possible.

Contact: Bill Vincent at rwgpublishing@yahoo.com